SHIPS

TRANSPORTATION

David and Patricia Armentrout

Rourke
Publishing LLC
Vero Beach, Florida 32964

www.rourkepublishing.com

PHOTO CREDITS: ©DigitalVision, LLC Cover, pp. 4, 8, 15, 17; ©Carnival Cruise Lines Title page; ©Louisiana Office of Tourism pp. 7, 21; ©PhotoDisc, Inc. p. 13; ©Queen Mary p. 10; ©United States Navy p. 18.

Title page: *The* Conquest *cruise ship departs from New Orleans and sails the western Caribbean.*

Editor: Frank Sloan

Cover design by Nicola Stratford

Library of Congress Cataloging-in-Publication Data

Armentrout, David, 1962-
  Ships / David and Patricia Armentrout.
      p. cm. — (Transportation)
Includes bibliographical references and index.
Contents: Ships and shipping — Powering ships — Ferryboats — Ocean liners — Cruise ships — Cargo ships — Container ships and tankers — Aircraft carriers — Ships at work — Dates to remember.
  ISBN 1-58952-671-6 (hardcover)
  1. Ships—Juvenile literature. [1. Ships.] I. Armentrout, Patricia, 1960- II. Title. III. Series: Armentrout, David,   1962- Transportation.

VM150.A73 2003
623.8'2—dc21

2003007276

Printed in the USA

CG/CG

Table of Contents

Ships and Shipping

A ship is a large vessel that travels on water. The term boat describes a small water vessel, although some large water vessels are called boats, such as ferryboats.

Shipping is the **industry** that moves people and **cargo** by water. There are many kinds of ships, from cruise ships to oil tankers.

Powering Ships

Early ships were powered by man, then by wind using sails. The invention of the steam engine greatly improved how ships transported people and cargo.

American inventor Robert Fulton built a steamboat in 1807. Steamboats have flat bottoms and travel well in lakes and rivers. A steam engine powers a paddle wheel, which **propels** the boat. Steamboats are still in use, but **diesel** and **gas turbine** engines power most ships today. Most modern ships are driven by propellers.

The Mississippi Queen *is a modern version of a steamboat.*

Ferryboats

A ferryboat travels short distances, usually in calm waters such as rivers and bays. Ferries transport passengers and cargo. Car ferries transport passengers and vehicles. The vehicles are driven onto a lower deck and parked.

Some ferryboats are hydrofoils. A hydrofoil rises out of the water as it increases speed. The foils are attached to the hull and act like wings, keeping the hull above water. Hydrofoils go much faster than ordinary ships.

Ferryboat passengers enjoy the view from the upper deck.

Ocean Liners

Ocean liners were huge ships that ran regular ocean routes during the early to mid 1900s. Ocean liners carried passengers and some cargo.

The *Queen Mary* is a British liner that was launched in 1934. In 1938, she (ships are often called "she") won the Blue Riband, a trophy given for the fastest North Atlantic crossing. The *Queen Mary* made 1,001 **transatlantic** trips before she was taken out of service in 1967. She is now a hotel and museum in Long Beach, California.

The Queen Mary *arrives in New York on its first voyage in 1936.*

Cruise Ships

The rise of airline service in the 1950s took passenger business away from ocean liners. Airlines offered passengers lower fares and faster service.

Today, cruise ships have replaced the ocean liner. Cruise ships visit popular vacation spots such as the Caribbean, the Mediterranean, and Alaska.

A cruise ship offers many comforts. For example, many large ships have bedroom suites, restaurants, a movie theater, pools, and a fitness room and spa.

A cruise ship is docked in San Diego's harbor.

Cargo Ships

The increase in airline service in the 1950s did not hurt the cargo shipping business. Cargo ships hold much more than planes, and shipping large quantities by water costs less than by air.

Cargo ships haul goods all over the world. Cargo ships carry everything from lumber and coal to manufactured goods like clothing and furniture. Cargo ships are sometimes called bulk carriers or freighters.

Powerful cranes are used to load lumber onto the deck of this cargo ship.

Container Ships and Tankers

Container ships carry standard-sized containers packed with a variety of goods. The containers are loaded and unloaded by giant cranes and are easily transferred to trains or trucks where they are taken to their final destination.

A tanker ship is built to carry liquid cargo, such as petroleum, or oil. Oil tankers are the largest cargo ships in the world and can haul more than 300,000 tons (272,155 metric tons) of oil.

A tugboat moves this container ship close to its dock.

Aircraft Carriers

   Aircraft carriers are the largest military ships in the world. They transport cargo, aircraft, and a crew of thousands.

   The U.S.S. *Nimitz*, for example, is 1,092 feet (332 meters) long. It can carry up to 6,000 people and 90 aircraft. The aircraft are stored below deck. The Nimitz is a **nuclear-powered** ship. It can operate at sea for about 70 days before restocking supplies.

The U.S.S. Nimitz *sails the waters of northern Canada.*

Ships at Work

People build boats and ships in all shapes and sizes. Some are used for recreation. Others, such as barges and fishing boats, make work easier. Still others are built as research ships that help us explore the deep blue sea.

People depend on boats and ships for transportation. Without them, it would be impossible to live the way we do today.

Barges carry cargo on rivers just like trucks carry cargo on roads.

Dates to Remember

1807   Robert Fulton builds the first successful
        steamboat
1934   British ocean liner *Queen Mary* is
        launched
1938   *Queen Mary* wins the Blue Riband trophy
1956   First passenger hydrofoil goes into
        operation
1967   *Queen Mary* is taken out of service
1972   The U.S.S. *Nimitz* is launched

Glossary

cargo (KAR goh) — goods carried by ships, trucks, or airplanes

container (kun TAY nuhr) — a covering for shipping cargo

diesel (DEE zuhl) —a fuel that is heavier than gasoline

gas turbine (GASS TUR bine) — an engine driven by gas passing through blades of a wheel and making it revolve

industry (IN duh stree) — companies or businesses of the same type

nuclear-powered (NOO klee ur POW urd) — energy created by splitting atoms

propels (pruh PELZ) — drives or pushes something

transatlantic (tran suht LAN tik) — crossing the Atlantic Ocean

Index

Further Reading

Batio, Christopher. *Super Cargo Ships*. Motorbooks International, 2001

Francis, Dorothy. *Our Transportation Systems*. The Millbrook Press, 2002

Gibbons, Tony. *The Encyclopedia of Ships*. Thunder Bay Press, 2001

Websites To Visit

www.queenmary.com/

www.navy.mil/homepages/cvn68/main.htm

www.deltaqueen.com/

About The Authors

David and Patricia Armentrout have written many nonfiction books for young readers on a variety of subjects. They have had several books published for primary school reading. The Armentrouts live in Cincinnati, Ohio, with their two children.

DISCARD